PERFORMANCE MONITORING OF
MICRO-CONTRACTS

FOR THE PROCUREMENT OF URBAN INFRASTRUCTURE

PERFORMANCE MONITORING OF
MICRO-CONTRACTS
FOR THE PROCUREMENT OF URBAN INFRASTRUCTURE

M. Sohail and Andrew Cotton

Water, Engineering and Development Centre
Loughborough University
2000

Water, Engineering and Development Centre,
Loughborough University,
Leicestershire, LE11 3TU, UK

© Water, Engineering and Development Centre Loughborough University 2000

ISBN 13 Paperback: 978 0 90605 570 0
ISBN Ebook: 9781788533218
Book DOI: http://dx.doi.org/10.3362/9781788533218

A catalogue record for this book is available from the British Library.

A reference copy of this publication is also available online at:
http://www.lboro.ca.uk/pmmc/contents.htm

Sohail, M. and Cotton, A.P. (2000)
Performance Monitoring of Micro-contracts for the
Procurment of Urban Infrastructure
WEDC, Loughborough University UK.

WEDC (The Water, Engineering and Development Centre) at Loughborough University in the UK is one of the world's leading institutions concerned with education, training, research and consultancy for the planning, provision and management of physical infrastructure for development in low- and middleincome countries.

This edition is reprinted and distributed by Practical Action Publishing.
Since 1974, Practical Action Publishing has published and disseminated books and information in support of international development work throughout the world. Practical Action Publishing trades only in support of its parent charity objectives and any profits are covenanted back to Practical Action (Charity Reg. No. 247257, Group VAT Registration No. 880 9924 76).

All reasonable precautions have been taken by the WEDC, Loughborough University to verify the information contained in this publication. However, WEDC, Loughborough University does not necessarily endorse the technologies presented in this document. The published material is being distributed without warranty of any kind, either expressed or implied. The responsibility for the interpretation and use of the material lies with the reader. In no event shall the WEDC, Loughborough University be liable for damages as a result of their use.

This document is an output from a project funded by the UK Department for International Development (DFID) for the benefit of low-income countries.
The views expressed are not necessarily those of DFID.

About the Authors

Dr M. Sohail is a Research Manager at WEDC. A specialist in urban services management, some of his recent research includes micro-contracts, procurement, project management, public-private partnerships, operation and maintenance and public transport.

Dr Andrew Cotton is the Director of Urban Programmes at WEDC. A specialist in urban infrastructure for low-income countries, some of his recent research includes micro-contracts, operation and maintenance, knowledge management and urban sanitation.

Acknowledgements

The authors gratefully acknowledge the many different people who have willingly contributed their knowledge and their time to the development of this work.

In particular we wish to thank Mr G Ganepola, National Housing Development Authority, Sri Lanka; Mr Chularathne, Sevenatha, Colombo, Sri Lanka; Mr Kevin Tayler, GHK Research and Training, UK; Ms Jo Beall, London Scool of Economics, UK; Mr Noman Ahmed, Dawood Engineering College, Karachi, Pakistan; Participants from India attending 'Community based infrastructure' training programmes funded by DFID (India); Mr Tasneem Siddiqui, Sindh Katchi Abadi Authority; Mr Arif Hassan, Consultant to OPP; Mr Shahid Mehmood, Community Action Programme; Mr Attaullah Khan, Faisalabad Area Upgrading Programme; Faisalabad Development Authority; Mr N.A. Watoo Anjuman-e-Samaji Behbood, Faislabad; Ms Perveen Rehmnan, Director OPP; Mr Saleem Aleem-ud-din, Director OPP; and Mr Brian Baxendale, Water and Sanitation Office, DFID India.

Contents

Section 1
Introduction

Project details

This document presents the findings from Project R6857 *Performance Monitoring of Infrastructure Procurement for Urban Low Income Communities* carried out by the authors as part of the Knowledge and Research Programme, Infrastructure and Urban Development Department, Department for International Development (DFID) of the British Government.

Purpose

The purpose of this project is to develop a framework and tools for the appraisal, monitoring and evaluation of micro-contracts for the procurement of local infrastructure in urban low income communities. In addition to the standard measures of time, cost and quality, the work also attempts to capture some of the crucial wider socio-economic impacts of community-based works. The findings in this booklet will be of use to donor/lending agencies, government officials, and non-government organisations (NGOs) involved in improving services for the urban poor.

Background

Procurement is the process of buying the goods, works or services, which in our case comprise local infrastructure in urban neighbourhoods. In engineering terms, the works themselves are minor and usually of low cost, but are nevertheless complex to implement given the physical and social fabric of low income urban areas. We adopt the term *micro-contract* to refer to the countless number of small contracts for works which are the mainstay of urban improvement in South Asia. The contract value is typically less than £10,000, and the duration less than one year.

A recent research project funded by DFID explored the issues surrounding local procurement of infrastructure. This focused on the various options for community involvement in the procurement process and on the different procedures and rules which govern public sector works (See *Community Initiatives in Urban Infrastructure* by Cotton et al, 1998). One of the findings of this research was that there was a need to provide policy makers and practitioners with tools for assessing the performance of micro contracts. These tools need to address the traditional concerns with time, cost and quality but must also capture wider economic and social impacts of community-based works. The present research project was accordingly funded by DFID to explore these issues.

The project objectives are thus very much about developing information systems that can be used in decision-making by the various target groups. These include the measures of time, cost and quality and the wider impacts relating to empowerment and socio economic benefits which may result when community groups are partners in the process of infrastructure procurement.

Possible benefits relating to the empowerment of community members might include:

- improved access to information, leading to a better understanding of their situation and the options open to them;
- increased ability to negotiate, identify opportunities and resolve conflicts, both within the community and with external stakeholders; and
- increased opportunities for the participation or representation of community members in decision-making processes.

Key issues in relation to potential socio-economic benefits are:

- the extent to which various forms of procurement provide direct and indirect economic benefits to community members; and
- the ways in which those benefits are distributed.

Direct economic benefits include the income that accrues to community members through their involvement in the procurement process, and reductions in the financial cost of facilities because of this involvement. Against the latter must be set the possible opportunity cost of time required for community-based approaches to infrastructure provision, for instance that spent in meetings and in providing labour and management inputs.

About this document
The results of our investigations are presented in this document. Section 2 contains the framework for performance assessment, and Section 3 presents the tested performance indicators and guidelines on how to use them. This will be of direct use to the target audiences as follows.

- Those responsible for managing the improvements to the performance of procurement of small scale infrastructure both in terms of contract performance and in achieving wider poverty related objectives; the likely target groups include senior local engineers, local programme managers and sector managers (both infrastructure and community development) of donor agency programmes.
- Those involved with the actual monitoring of performance both in terms of contract performance and in achieving wider poverty related objectives; the likely target groups include local executive engineers, local community development officers, and NGO groups involved in facilitating the procurement of community level services.

Section 4 contains the supporting evidence for our findings; this includes a summary of data obtained during field testing, and a case study report. This will be of interest principally to other researchers; however, some of the material will be directly relevant to the audiences described above as and when they need to explore some of the issues arising in more detail.

Research methodology

This research explores approximately 800 micro-contracts awarded by urban local authorities, special projects and NGOs in south Asia. These contracts covered both conventional tender contract and community partnered procurement processes (Cotton et al, 1998). The first stage involved the collection of background information through:

- a review of literature, documents and project files on urban infrastructure in India, Pakistan and Sri Lanka;
- interviews; and
- focus group discussions.

The second stage was the development of draft indicators to explore the performance of both conventional and community partnered contracts used in the procurement of infrastructure. These were developed from the literature review, interviews and focus group discussions, and were distributed to over 200 individuals for comment.

The indicators were field tested in the study countries in relation to:

- programmes initiated by community based organizations (CBOs) and (NGOs);

- works carried out by municipal government; and
- donor funded urban development programmes.

The indicators were tested on a variety of micro-contracts relating to urban infrastructure. These include water and sanitation (including solid waste), access related works, drainage, small buildings and parks. Subsequently, amendments were discussed during a regional workshop in Nepal in 1998 and in a workshop in Lusaka in 1999.

The indicators presented later in this document incorporate the comments received on the draft indicators, comments received during field testing, and issues raised in the regional and country workshops.

Summary findings

1. Indicators for measuring the performance of micro contracts in the procurement of urban infrastructure are grouped as follows:

   - *general;*
   - *time;*
   - *cost;*
   - *quality of work;*
   - *inter-organizational co-operation and partnership; and*
   - *socio-economic issues.*

2. *General, time, cost* and *quality of work* indicators apply to all contracts; for community partnered works indicators relating to *inter-organizational co-operation and partnership* and *socio-economic issues* are also relevant.

3. For the contracts considered in this study the following overall averages for cost growth and time growth were obtained for the community and non-community partnered contracts:

Cost growth (community)	=	1.02
Cost growth (non-community)	=	1.01
Time growth (community)	=	1.64
Time growth (non-community)	=	1.39

   This suggests that costs are kept under tight control, but that there is less control on time overruns.

4

4. Indicators dealing with the participation of women and disadvantaged groups reveal that in many cases no specific action was taken to ensure such participation.

5. It was found important to differentiate between the formal and informal meetings and training; for example, it appears that women may benefit more from informal training. In some cases users of the indicators had difficulty in obtaining information related to informal training days.

6. It is important to identify not only the number of meetings with the community, but also the quality of those meetings; the atmosphere, level of participation and impacts.

7. The number of community labour days generated by micro-contracts injects significant money into the local economy; note that this indicator is useful in non-community partnered works as well as community-partnered works.

8. It is very difficult to assess the quality of construction work in an objective manner using performance indicators. The opinions of the users of the improved services is the critical component here; this requires further investigation using participatory techniques. More attention needs to be paid to monitoring of quality. Possible ways forward include the beneficiary community groups themselves engaging advisory technical staff and increasing the direct involvement of user groups themselves in supervision of work.

9. As a general guide to using these indicators:

   • at the outset, select a limited number of indicators which give information about overall performance in areas which are relevant to the local situation;
   • these will identify the key problem areas which can then be explored in more detail through the careful selection of further indicators.

Reference
Cotton, A.P., Sohail, M. and Tayler, W.K. (1998) *Community Initiatives in Urban Infrastructure*. WEDC, Loughborough University, UK.

Section 2
Framework for performance monitoring

What this section will tell you
This section will tell you about three important things:

- the reasons why it is important to monitor performance;
- the need for a framework for performance monitoring; a suitable framework is presented and described; and
- the different types of performance indicators and the ways in which they can be used within the overall framework.

Finally, the concept of benchmarking is discussed and some benchmark values for selected key indicators are presented.

Why monitor performance?
Performance monitoring is a valuable management tool for highlighting successes and failures in the procurement process, and for identifying key areas for improvements. In addition to the traditional areas of time, cost, and quality of work, potential improvements in the socio-economic impacts of community-partnered procurement may also be identified. Armed with measures of performance, managers are in a position to formulate policy and implement plans which are relevant to the problems which are exposed, and conversely to avoid action that is unnecessary. Performance monitoring needs to take place against a number of clearly defined *indicators*; performance targets can be developed for a particular period and in the local context which enable managers to identify areas for improvements.

A framework for performance monitoring
Any improvement in the performance of micro-contracts depends on the existence of a management system within which performance improvements can take place; this leads to a 'virtuous circle' of improvement as shown in Figure 2.1.

The key point underlying all of this is that action will be taken as a result of measuring performance in a particular area of activity, which in our case is that of infrastructure procurement. It is important to understand that in some cases the basic management structures at the institutional level are underdeveloped, and it is difficult both to gather relevant information on performance and from that to develop action plans to improve performance.

The focus of this work is on two of the above stages, namely:

- the framework for performance measurement; and
- the measurement and reporting of performance.

The more detailed framework shown in Figure 2.2 outlines a number of stages in the process for measuring and evaluating the effectiveness of infrastructure procurement (after MDF 1993; WHO 2000).

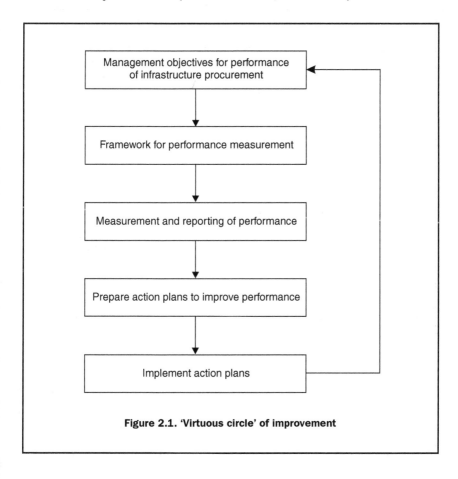

Figure 2.1. 'Virtuous circle' of improvement

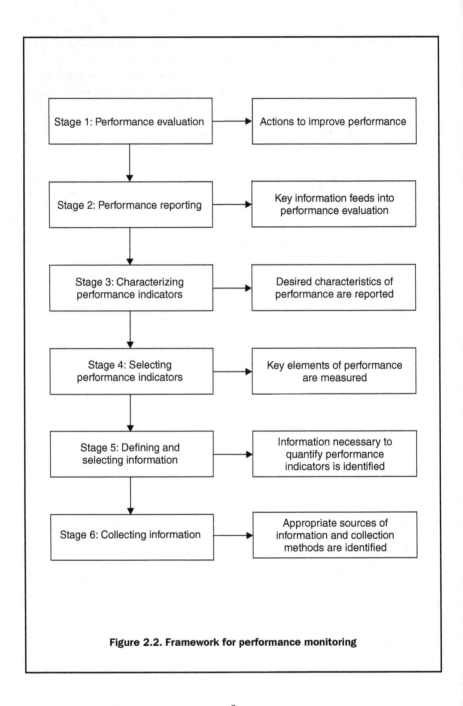

Figure 2.2. Framework for performance monitoring

8

Each of these stages is described in more detail in the following boxes.

Stage 1: Performance evaluation

Commentary

Action Plans to improve infrastructure procurement need to be based on a sound evaluation of performance of different methods of procurement. Performance evaluation needs to answer specific questions which are relevant to those in a position to take action relating to infrastructure procurement, whether it be using conventional tender contract systems or by involving the local communities.

Performance evaluation needs to take place against a number of clearly defined criteria or targets which have been set for a particular reporting period and within the local context. The approach adopted is to define performance indicators having quantitative or qualitative values which cover the field of infrastructure procurement. Associated with each performance indicator is a performance target; the status, or 'performance', of the procurement process is then assessed by comparing each performance indicator with its respective target. This enables performance comparisons to be made:

- between different time periods for a given procurement process; and
- between different methods of procurement.

This document does not attempt to prescribe arbitrary performance targets; these must be developed within the local context. However, benchmark values are presented for a number of selected key indicators.

Key points
- Action plans to improve the process of infrastructure procurement need to be based on an evaluation of actual performance.
- Evaluation needs to be based on the use of indicators and targets.

Stage 2: Performance reporting

Commentary

Performance reporting provides the essential input to performance evaluation. It not only reveals whether planned actions have achieved their objectives, but identifies common problems and allows improvements to be built into the system for the future. The development of a sound performance reporting system along with the choice of appropriate performance indicators are important elements in the evaluation of the infrastructure procurement process.

Key points

Investigate what are the existing performance reporting systems, and whether they are sufficiently well developed to permit a thorough evaluation of the procurement process to be carried out.

Stage 3: Characterizing performance indicators

Commentary
Performance indicators can be defined as *variables whose purpose is to measure change in a process or function.* They provide the information from which performance reports are compiled, in order to assist in answering the questions posed by performance evaluation of the infrastructure procurement process. Performance indicators should be selected based on managerial requirements.

Characteristics of a good performance indicator are:
*   a valid link between the indicator and the question being addressed; will problems be detected by the use of the indicator?
*   does the indicator give an idea of the magnitude of the problem?
*   the information required to define the indicator is readily available.

Information relevant to the procurement process can usefully be grouped as follows:
*   general;
*   time;
*   cost;
*   quality;
*   inter-organizational co-operation and partnership;
*   socio-economic issues e.g. enterprise development, poverty alleviation and empowerment.

Key points
*   When setting up performance indicators make sure that they display the appropriate characteristic; use the above groupings as a starting point to focus attention on the key areas.
*   See Section 3 for further details on how to develop performance indicators and descriptions of the different groupings of indicators.

Stage 4: Selecting performance indicators for the procurement process

Commentary
There is no fixed set of questions which can be applied to all situations; the indicators selected will be different for conventional tender contract systems and community partnered procurement processes. These will vary from place to place according to the local context. Once the indicators have been selected, check that they will assist in answering the important questions about the infrastructure procurement process.

Key points
*   It is essential to think about what a particular indicator is telling you; can the information be used as the basis for actions.

- Avoid collecting large amounts of data (either through objective means or using participatory techniques) which cannot subsequently be put to the intended purpose.
- Select appropriate performance indicators from Section 3.

Stage 5: Defining and selecting information

Commentary
The nature and form of the information systems is crucially important for determining performance indicators and developing performance reports. We must know:
- what information needs to be collected in relation to each indicator; and
- where that information can be found.

This requires a careful review of the different indicators in order to see whether or not information will be readily available, and if necessary to plan for the collection of the information required. Some information may require processing before it can be used as an indicator.

Key points
- For conventional micro-contracts, information about the procurement process should be available through a management information system; in some cases this may be poorly developed or non-existent.
- For community partnered procurement, the key knowledge lies with the community of users and may not be recorded in a formal sense.
- The tables of performance indicators in Section 3 suggest likely sources of information for each indicator.

Stage 6: Collecting the information

Commentary
This is more complex than appears at first sight as there are two distinct methods which can be employed.
- Performance indicators which can be assessed in an objective manner by collection of performance data; this could be done internally using the staff of the institution or by using external consultants.
- Performance indicators based on qualitative information; this often requires either processing of available data or collection of new data using participatory assessments of performance.

Key points
- Distinguish clearly between indicators which require different data collection methodologies.
- The tables of performance indicators in Section 3 suggest likely sources of information for each indicator.

11

More about performance indicators

A performance indicator can be defined as an item of information that is collected to record some aspect of an activity or a system. Everyone uses indicators but this is rarely made explicit in everyday life. For instance, someone who is having an extension built to their house may request quotes from two or more builders. The final decision on which builder to choose is likely to depend on a number of considerations, in particular the price, but also including less definite considerations such as the builder's reputation, recommendations from previous clients and perhaps just personal impressions. None of this, apart possibly from the prices, will be written down and formally analysed but a decision will nevertheless be reached. Such indicators can be said to be informal.

The essential point about the indicators used by an individual for his or her own purposes is that they have at most to be communicated to a small number of stakeholders, in most cases only the immediate family. This means that there is no need to record them. The same applies to indicators used by small groups of people when there are strong relationships of trust. As the size of the group increases and relationships become more impersonal, the need to have clearly defined systems for assessing activities becomes greater. So the indicators used by governments and international agencies must be clearly defined, accessible and transparent. We are concerned here primarily with these more formal indicators although it should be recognised that the systems used by people at the community level should not be too different from the informal systems with which people are familiar.

Quantitative and qualitative indicators

Indicators may be quantitative or qualitative in nature. The average cost incurred and the time taken to complete a particular item of work are both quantitative indicators. In contrast, a community member's perception of his or her satisfaction with the results of a particular community procurement process is essentially qualitative in nature. For comparison purposes, it will usually be necessary to find some way of placing some quantitative value on such qualitative indicators. It is arguable that processes that cannot be measured cannot be managed. This statement might be questioned by a group that combines together to provide some basic item of shared infrastructure but it is true that in some way they measure costs against perceived benefits. It is certainly widely accepted by governments and international agencies that quantitative information is needed if choices are to be made between a range of possible development options. A common response to the need to quantify indicators is the use of ranking scales in which for instance the person's satisfaction with a process, activity or situation might be ranked on a scale ranging from very happy, through happy, indifferent and unhappy to very unhappy. Such ranking scales must be set up at the time that indicators are identified and introduced to an overall monitoring and evaluation system.

Process and output indicators

Indicators may relate to processes and the outcomes from those processes. Process indicators may relate to both the **quality** of the process and its **progress**. Indicators relating to the quality of a process might cover such questions as 'who is involved?', 'what role are they playing?' and 'what are the power relationships within the group?'. Those relating to progress will be concerned primarily with the question 'is the process occurring as planned?'. Information on the quality of a process can be used by managers as the basis on which to amend and improve that process. It can also be used to assess the outcomes of that process and the possibility that this assessment may lead to changes in the design of future initiatives. Indicators of progress are immediately useful to the managers of a project or process but they may also help in the assessment of the efficacy of that process.

Indicators relating to outcomes are primarily required to assess the success of projects and to measure their achievements. They are intended to help planners to determine the extent to which the project or process achieved its objectives. At the project level, the concern will be with whether it has achieved both its specified outputs and its overall purpose. At a wider level, there is a need to consider the overall impact of projects and programmes on fundamental indicators, for instance those that measure the level of poverty in a society.

Check what the performance indicator will tell you

When choosing performance indicators for infrastructure procurement, the following factors need to be taken into account for a performance indicator PI(x) which is intended to measure the performance of X.

Evaluating performance indicators
- Is X an area which falls under the control of the user?
- Will the PI(x) measure what is needed?
- Will problems in area X be detected by the use of PI(x)?
- Does PI(x) give an idea of the magnitude of the problem?
- Is data available to compute PI(x)?
- Is PI(x) accepted by the people involved?
- Are there any other indicators that can help identify the cause of the problem?
- Who will use PI(x)?

Performance indicators in monitoring and evaluation

Performance indicators are normally used in one of two ways. They may be collected at regular intervals to track the way in which a system is performing or an activity is unfolding. Alternatively, they may be used to assess the change resulting from a particular activity or project. In the first case, they are being used to **monitor** the progress of a process, while in the latter their purpose is to **evaluate** the outcome of a project or process. Evaluation requires that the situation is assessed both at the beginning and at the end of the project or process. This suggests that there is a need to collect baseline data relating to the proposed performance indicators before a project or process starts. Information collected before a project or process begins can and should also be used to inform decisions on what is to be done. This information should, wherever possible, include data taken from previous initiatives so that lessons from the past can inform the new venture.

These uses of indicators are strongly linked with the project cycle of identification, implementation, operation and assessment. The use of information to inform decisions is an essential aspect of project identification. Monitoring systems are required to ensure that implementation and operation proceed as planned and to provide the basis for corrective action if there is a problem. As already indicated, process indicators will be important in this respect. Evaluation systems are required in order to assess the achievements and impact of a project or programme. Evaluation requires the assessment of change and hence is dependent on the existence of adequate baseline information; this in turn means that performance indicators should be in place at the beginning of any initiative. Timeliness in the development and application of indicators is essential.

Performance indicators and planning

Indicators can be used by a range of stakeholders to assist them in planning projects, programmes and policies. It starts from the assumption that the evaluation of completed projects, programmes and policies should provide an input into plans for the future. In effect, evaluation of what has gone before becomes part of the appraisal process for what is to come.

Most of the indicators presented in this study are concerned with performance at the level of the individual contract. However, it is important to recognise that, when brought together and analysed, the information obtained through such indicators can be important in shaping programmes and policies. For instance, indicators of the local employment resulting from specific schemes featuring community-partnered procurement might provide a strong rationale for the development of changes in policy to encourage

14

such partnerships. A related point is that, while individual schemes may result in improvements in the local situation, assessment of the cumulative effect of a number of projects is necessary if overall impacts of different approaches to infrastructure provision are to be assessed.

Professionals involved in infrastructure provision have traditionally been interested in the efficiency with which facilities have been provided. Their concern has been with the cost of works, the time taken to complete them and their quality. As already indicated in Section 1, the research has taken a wider perspective, exploring indicators that relate to the 'softer' impacts of infrastructure procurement. Some of these impacts are sensitive to the process of procurement; some are process independent.

Key points when using performance indicators

To summarise, the following points need to be kept in mind when using performance indicators.

- They should be truly representative of the quantities and characteristics that they are intended to represent.
- They should be verifiable; in other words, it should be possible to check that the values of the data or indicators presented are accurately reported.
- They should provide information that can be used by decision-makers. As already indicated, this will often mean that they are presented quantitatively.
- The information must be available in time to influence decisions.
- They should be linked into systems that allow feedback of information into the decision-making process.

Benchmarking

Benchmarking is a tool for continuous improvement that to date has mainly been used in the context of the commercial private sector. However, there is no reason why the concept could not be applied to public sector procurement of infrastructure and services for low income urban communities. A benchmark is a position against which performance can be measured; valuable resources can then be targeted to those areas requiring the greatest improvement. In our case, the benchmark position is the level of performance of contracts in the delivery of infrastructure and services to low income urban communities. The idea is to surpass the best level and hence create continuous improvement.

Establishment of a yardstick or benchmarks for micro-contracts in the public sector will make it feasible to monitor the performance of such contracts within a single organization or between organizations.

The performance of both micro-contracts and the procurement process can be benchmarked. The main approach that can be used is as follows:

- study and understand ones' own process;
- find the best benchmarking partners;
- study the partners' process;
- analyze the difference between ones' own and ones' partners process; and
- implement improvements based on what is learned from the benchmarking partner.

The data collected during the field testing of the indicators has been used to provide benchmark values for a number of selected indicators. These are presented in Table 2.1. Separate values are shown for conventional and community partnered contracts, although an overall figure is also given within the remarks. The figures have been based on the best average value from individual organizations.

Key to performance indicators selected for benchmarking

Performance indicator	Description
R1	Cost growth = Final contract cost/Initial contract cost
R2	Time growth = Final contract duration/Initial contract duration
R3	Lead time = Time required to commence works/contract duration
R4	Technical sanction cost/Engineer's detailed estimate
R5	Engineer's detailed estimate/Initial contract cost
R6	Engineer's detailed estimate/Final contract cost
TL1	Time taken from approval to Tender invitation
TL6	Time taken from approval to the start of the contract
TL9	Time taken to commence O&M after completion of the contract
TL13	Time taken from Tender invitation to the start of the contract

References

MDF, (1993) 'Design of a Project Monitoring System', Training Notes, Ede, The Netherlands.

WHO, (2000) *Operation and Maintenance of Urban Water Supply and Sanitation Systems*, WHO, Geneva.

Table 2.1. Proposed benchmark values for selected indicators

Items	Benchmarks non-community	Benchmarks community	Remarks
R1	1.04	1.08	Target to keep the cost within +/- 8%
R2	1.58	1.31	Target not to overrun the contract by more than 50%
R3	0.54	0.64	Target not to take more than 50% of the contract duration for preparation
R4	1.02	1.03	Target: estimates within 3%
R5	1.01	1.02	Target: estimates within 2%
R6	1.05	1.01	Target: estimates within 5%
TL1	32	28	Say one month
TL6	35	31	Say one month
TL9	31	17	Say two weeks
TL13	32	40	Six weeks

Section 3
Guidelines: The performance indicators and how to use them

What this section will tell you

This section describes the way in which the indicators are grouped and provides guidance on the selection of relevant indicators by means of two flow charts. Finally, the indicators themselves are presented in a series of tables. These guidelines do not propose a step by step methodology leading to guaranteed success; we are dealing with a process and local circumstances will dictate the way in which the indicators are used.

Performance monitoring indicators for micro-contracts

Sixty nine indicators were developed and tested during this study, covering aspects of the complete life-cycle of a typical contract: planning and design, implementation, post-completion and operation and maintenance. However, please note that you need not use all the indicators at any one time. You should develop your own priority and selection systems depending on the key objectives of your performance monitoring. In short, the indicators should be taken as a flexible set of tools that can be used readily, developed further or discarded depending on the objectives of the performance monitoring.

Suggested grouping of performance indicators

It is useful to group the performance indicators into the following six general categories which relate to the nature of the information which the indicators are describing:

- general;
- time;
- cost;
- quality;
- inter-organizational co-operation and partnership; and
- socio-economic issues.

These are discussed further below.

General

It is useful to have an overview of some of the fundamental aspects of a particular contract , for example who initiated the works; the degree of community involvement; and who has responsibility for operation and maintenance. A number of indicators are presented covering issues of ownership, roles and responsibilities and power relations.

Time

Delays may occur at different stages of the procurement process depending on the method of procurement, the management systems in place, and/or the personnel involved. Performance indicators can measure the time performance of the procurement process at different stages of the contract. Avoidable delays may be identified and measures put in place to reduce these in the future.

Cost

In South Asia the cost of the work is generally estimated at several stages of the procurement process:

- a preliminary estimate prepared using 'rule of thumb' methods;
- a cost estimate prepared by the Engineer, based on a Schedule of Rates (Technical Sanction Cost);
- a more detailed cost estimate prepared by the Engineer at the tender stage; and
- the initial contract cost (the Contractors' estimate for carrying out the work).

Performance indicators can be selected to monitor the relationship between the Engineers' and Contractors' estimates and the final cost of the contract.

Quality

If the work carried out by the Contractor does not meet the required standard it will be rejected. A single indicator based on the number of times when work was rejected is proposed as a measure of quality performance. However, in many situations, truly independent valuations of quality may be lacking, and it is valuable to investigate this as part of an in depth participatory assessment (see Section 4).

Inter-organizational co-operation and partnership

The ways in which officials and the community interact, and the degree of co-operation between them, can significantly affect the efficiency and success of a project.

Socio-economic issues

In addition to the infrastructure itself a community may receive a number of other benefits as a result of infrastructure procurement. These may relate to skills development through training, increased employment and empowerment.

Guidance points

There are two fundamental questions which must be answered before the process of selecting the relevant indicators can begin:

- what type of contract are you dealing with (conventional or community partnered)?
- what aspects of performance do you want to measure?

The answers to these questions will determine which groups of indicators should be considered. The flow charts (Figures 3.1 and 3.2) guide the reader through this process.

In terms of guiding you in the actual application and use of the indicators, we present the indicators in three parts (A-C):

Part-A   General performance monitoring of micro-contracts.

Part-B   Inter-organizational co-operation and partnership.

Part-C   Socio-economic issues related to enterprise development, poverty alleviation and empowerment.

Part A is suitable for monitoring both community partnered and conventional micro-contracts and is divided into four tables:

- general;
- time;

20

- cost; and
- quality.

Parts B and C are more specific to community partnered contracts.

The indicators are presented in tabular form with a short description which includes the source of information typically available. This will help you to understand the purpose of the indicator and give some guidance on 'where' and 'how' to use it.

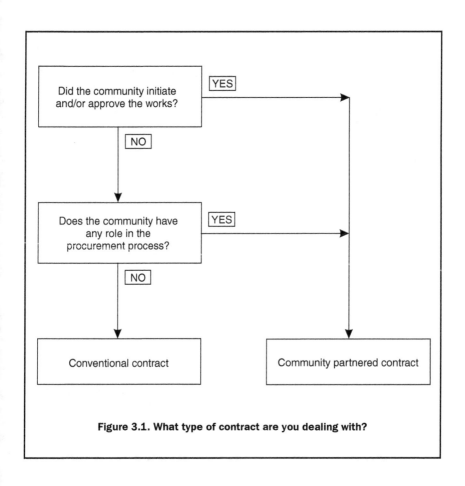

Figure 3.1. What type of contract are you dealing with?

21

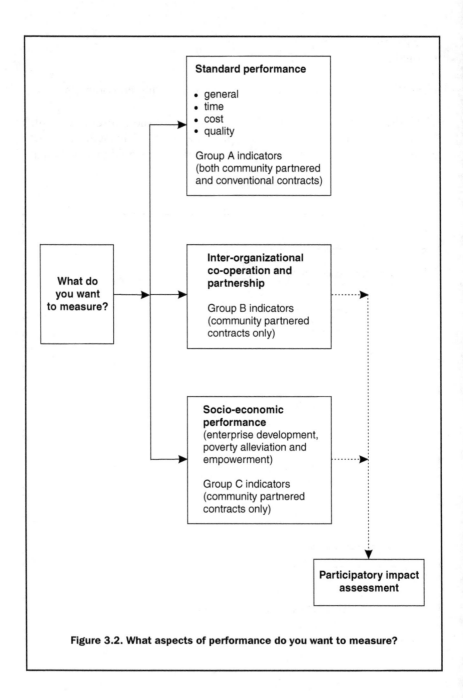

Figure 3.2. What aspects of performance do you want to measure?

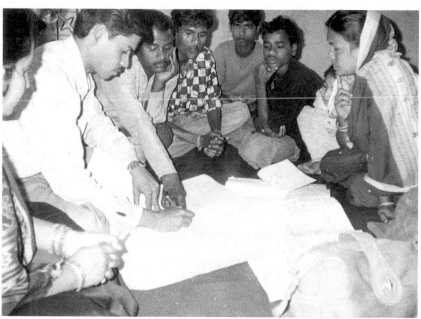

Part-A. General performance monitoring of micro-contracts

Table 3.1. General indicators

Indicator	Description
Handing/ taking over process: formal taking over by Maintenance agencies, defect liability period.	1. **Why:** who functionally owns the infrastructure, roles and responsibility and time period involved in someone taking over the assets. 2. **Key sources of information:** contract document, files, handing/taking over documents. 3. **How:** review of the documents and who is doing what after the completion of the works. Noting the date of completion and the end of defect liability period. Noting the date when the assets were taken over formally and informally. 4. **Comments:** issues of ownership, roles and responsibilities, risk distribution between parties. Who is responsible for the assets after completion. Who is responsible for executing operation and maintenance related activities.
Was the community involved in the O&M of the infrastructure?	1. **Why:** involvement of the community in operation and maintenance. 2. **Key sources of information:** key informants, observation and condition surveys of the assets. 3. **How:** interviews and review of the documents. 4. **Comments:** this relates to the manifestation of sense of ownership by the community and care of works and assets.
Number of disputes.	1. **Why:** this relates to the atmosphere of the working organization and the power relations.

	2. **Key sources of information:** contract files and key informants. 3. **How:** review of the documents and interviews. 4. **Comments:** this relates to the general working environment, partnering or adversarial, and to internal and external negotiation and conflict resolution.
Incidences of imposition of penalties/damages.	1. **Why:** power relations and seriousness in imposing damages. 2. **Key sources of information:** contract, contract files and key informants. 3. **How:** review of the documents and interviews. 4. **Comments:** this relates to power relations, and to the working environment.
Incidences of deviations and reasons for those.	1. **Why:** changes in the scope of work and other risks. 2. **Key sources of information:** contract files. 3. **How:** review of the documents. 4. **Comments:** this relates to the quality of the initial brief, attitude of the contractors and changing circumstances.
Incidences of delay in material supply, tools/plants [Departmental].	1. **Why:** performance of promoter in case of departmental works or labour contracts. 2. **Key sources of information:** site records and site supervisors. 3. **How:** interview and review of the documents. 4. **Comments:** responsibility of public sector if it is their activity.

Table 3.2. Time indicators

Indicator	Description
Incidences of applications for extra time and reasons for those.	1. **Why:** risks of time overruns and their reasons. 2. **Key sources of information:** contract files. 3. **How:** review of the documents. 4. **Comments:** relates to factors affecting the time performance.
Time growth (R2) = Final contract duration / Initial contract duration.	1. **Why:** performance of schedule control. 2. **Key sources of information:** contract files and key informants. 3. **How:** determine the initial and final contract duration. Divide the final contract duration by the initial contract duration. 4. **Comments:** this indicates the control of time schedule. Reasons for delays could be riots, rainy seasons or lack of performance of the contractor.
Lead time (R3) = Time required to reach the stage of commencement of works or services (TL6 or TL6A) / contract duration.	1. **Why:** promoter efficiency in contracting out the work. 2. **Key sources of information:** project file and key informants. 3. **How:** determine the time lag between the establishment of requirement and the contract commencement. Divide that time lag by the contract period. The units in which the duration is measured should be consistent. 4. **Comments:** this provides the time required to award the contract as a proportion of contract duration. The lead time is important in the overall delivery time of infrastructure. This indicator along with the time lags indicates the performance of the procurement process.

Time taken from approval stage to reach the tender inviting stage or equivalent stage (TL1).	1. **Why:** an indication of the time performance of the Promoter in the procurement process. 2. **Key sources of information:** project files and key informants. 3. **How:** determine the dates for approvals and invitation to tenders. Determine the difference between the dates. 4. **Comments:** this reflects the time performance of the promoter in reaching the stage of tender invitation. This time lag is important for the overall delivery time of the urban infrastructure.
Time taken from approval to contract stage (TL6).	1. **Why:** an indication of the time performance of the procurement process. 2. **Key sources of information:** project files and key informants. 3. **How:** determine the dates for approvals and contract start. Determine the difference between the dates. 4. **Comments:** the indicator reflects the time performance of the procurement process prior to the start of contract. The time taken to reach the contract stage is an important factor in overall delivery time of urban infrastructure.
Time taken between tender opening and tender approval (TL11).	1. **Why:** indicator of the time performance of the Promoter in the procurement process. 2. **Key sources of information:** project files. 3. **How:** determine the dates for tender opening and approval. Calculate the difference. 4. **Comments:** the pre-contract procurement process is divided into different stages. The overall delivery time of urban infrastructure is dependent on the performance of each element. This indicates the time performance of one such element.

...continued

Indicator	Description
Time taken between Tender invitation and start of contract (TL13).	1. **Why:** indicator of the time performance of the Promoter in the procurement process. 2. **Key sources of information:** project files, tender documents and key informants. 3. **How:** determine the dates for tender invitation and contract commencement. Calculate the difference. 4. **Comments:** the pre-contract procurement process is divided into different stages. The overall delivery time of urban infrastructure is dependent on the performance of each element. This indicates the time performance of one such element.
Time lag between tender opening and Technical sanction (TL14).	1. **Why:** indicator of the time performance of the Promoter in the procurement process. 2. **Key sources of information:** project files, tender documents. 3. **How:** determine the date for tender opening and the date for technical sanction. Calculate the difference. 4. **Comments:** the pre-contract procurement process is divided into different stages. The overall delivery time of urban infrastructure is dependent on the performance of each element. This indicates the time performance of one such element. This indicator may not be directly usable for processes that do not involve tendering. However, equivalencies could be found.

Time lag between the actual completion and the Technical sanction (TL15).	1. **Why:** indicator of the time performance of the Promoter in the procurement process. 2. **Key sources of information:** project files, contract documents and key informants. 3. **How:** determine the dates for actual completion and technical sanction. Calculate the difference. 4. **Comments:** the pre-contract procurement process is divided into different stages. The overall delivery time of urban infrastructure is dependent on the performance of each element. This indicates the time performance of one such element.	
Time lag between tender opening and Notice Inviting Tenders (TL16).	1. **Why:** indicator of the time performance of the Promoter in the procurement process. 2. **Key sources of information:** project files, tender documents and key informants. 3. **How:** determine the dates for tender opening and tender invitation. Calculate the difference. 4. **Comments:** the pre-contract procurement process is divided into different stages. The overall delivery time of urban infrastructure is dependent on the performance of each element. This indicates the time performance of one such element.	

29

...continued

Indicator	Description
Time taken between the contract start date and the actual start at site (TL8).	1. **Why:** time taken by the contractor to mobilize. 2. **Key sources of information:** contract files and key informants. 3. **How:** determine the contract start date and the physical start at site. Calculate the difference between those dates. 4. **Comments:** time lag between the work order and the actual start reflect the mobilization capacity of the contractor.
Time taken to start operation and maintenance after the contract is completed (TL9).	1. **Why:** reflects the measures of operation and maintenance and sustainability. 2. **Key sources of information:** contract documents, project files, handing and taking over documents and key informants. 3. **How:** determine the contract completion date and the date for taking over by the concerned agencies. In the case of informal and community contracts equivalent dates need to be determined. Calculate the difference between those dates. 4. **Comments:** taking over from the contractor indicates the time of start of, and responsibility for, operation and maintenance. If there is no arrangement for such taking over or operation and maintenance, the urban infrastructure may not be as sustainable.

Table 3.3. Cost indicators

Indicator	Description
Cost growth (R1) = Final contract cost / Initial contract cost.	1. Why: performance of cost control. 2. Key sources of information: contract files and key informants. 3. How: determine the costs at the start of contract and at the time of completion; divide the completion cost by the initial cost. 4. Comments: the ratio reflects the cost control used in the project. There may be many reasons for the high or low cost growth, for example political situation, inflation, climate but here we are focusing on the magnitude and not the reason.
Accuracy of preliminary technical estimates (R4) = Technical sanction cost / Engineer's detailed estimates.	1. Why: accuracy of the cost estimate. 2. Key sources of information: contract files and key informants. 3. How: determine the preliminary estimates and detailed Engineer's estimates. Divide the preliminary estimates by the detailed estimates. 4. Comments: This reflects on how good or bad the preliminary estimates are. The preliminary estimate is important as this dictates the approved cost of the project.
Proximity of Engineer's estimated cost and the initial contract cost (R5) = Engineer's detailed estimated cost / contract initial cost.	1. Why: to monitor the proximity of Engineer's estimates and the contract initial cost. 2. Key sources of information: tender document, project files and contract document. In the case of verbal or informal contracts equivalent information may be found from the key informants.

Indicator	Description
	3. **How:** determine the Engineer's estimated cost and the initial contract cost. Divide the Engineer's estimated cost by the initial contract cost. 4. **Comments:** the ratio reveals how close or otherwise the estimate is to the initial contract price. This government approved schedule of rates is the basis of the Engineer's estimates. This in turns also reflects the relevance of government rates to the market rates.
Proximity of Engineer's estimated cost and the final contract cost (R6) = Detailed estimated cost / completion cost.	1. **Why:** to monitor the proximity of Engineer's estimates and the final contract cost. 2. **Key sources of information:** tender document, project files and contract document. In the case of verbal or informal contracts equivalent information may be found from the key informants. 3. **How:** determine the Engineer's estimate and the final contract cost. Divide the estimated cost by the final contract cost. 4. **Comments:** The ratio reflects the accuracy of the estimates regarding the completion cost. This complements the idea of cost growth ratio (R1) above.

Table 3.4. Quality indicators

Indicator	Description
Incidences when the work was rejected.	1. **Why:** relates to quality control mechanism and power. 2. **Key sources of information:** site records, contract files, project memos and key site supervisors. 3. **How:** review of the documents and interviews. 4. **Comments:** relates to the quality , power relations and chain of communication.

Part-B. Inter-organizational co-operation and partnership

Table 3.5. Inter-organizational co-operation and partnership indicators

Indicator	Description
Documentation involved Any written contracts? Any standard conditions of contact? Was the contract verbal?	1. **Why:** degree of formality and associated barriers; this will indicate mode and form of communication and its suitability for use in the contract. 2. **Key sources of information:** documents and key informants. 3. **How:** review contract documents and consult key informants. 4. **Comments:** modes of communication indicate the level of formality and consequent implications for community access to the process of procurement at their given level of organization. This also indicates the behaviour of organizations involved in the procurement.
How the works commenced, any ceremonies etc.	1. **Why:** perceived importance of the work by the community. 2. **Key sources of information:** key informant and observation if the work is about to commence. 3. **How:** talking and observing. 4. **Comments:** social significance of the work attached by the community and the way people expressed their group feelings.
Community involvement in the decision making process: Who	1. **Why:** community power and authority in the decision making process.

were involved in deciding that the work was complete, determination of cost, satisfaction with quality?	2. **Key sources of information:** project notes, observation of community interactions, account of participation of community in different stages of decision making, key informants. 3. **How:** reviews and interviews. 4. **Comments:** issues of control, partnerships, transparency and power relations.
Number of FORMAL community meetings during: planning and design, implementation and post completion. Also mention the different groups that attended the meetings such as men, women, owners, renters, community leaders etc.	1. **Why:** an indication of interaction, information sharing and partnership. 2. **Key sources of information:** key informants and project files. 3. **How:** determine the number of formal meetings at different stages of the contract. 4. **Comments:** this will indicate the level of formal interaction from different parts of the community. This will also identify any dominant group in the community.
Number of INFORMAL community meetings during: planning and design, implementation and post completion. Also mention the different groups that attended the meetings such as men, women, owners, renters, community leaders etc.	1. **Why:** an indication of interaction, information sharing and partnership. 2. **Key sources of information:** project files and key informants. 3. **How:** determine the number of informal meetings at different stages of the contract. 4. **Comments:** informal meetings may be an important mode of communication and negotiation. This will indicate the level of informal interaction from different parts of the community and identify any dominant group.

...continued

Indicator	Description
Rank score the interaction between the officials and the community groups in the meeting during: planning and design, implementation and post completion [20 maximum and 10 minimum].	1. **Why:** monitor the level of interaction, transparency and information sharing. 2. **Key sources of information:** key informants and meeting notes, if any. 3. **How:** interviews and review of any documents. 4. **Comments:** this relates to qualitative aspects of a community meeting at a given stage.
Rank score community attendance during: planning and design, implementation and post completion [20 maximum attendance 10 minimum].	1. **Why:** monitor the level of community participation in the procurement process. 2. **Key sources of information:** key informants, observations and meeting minutes. 3. **How:** review of any documents and interviews. 4. **Comments:** this will indicate the variation of community participation at different stages of procurement.
Mention the different groups that attended the meetings such as men, women, owners, renters, community leaders etc. during: planning and design, implementation and post completion.	1. **Why:** monitor the quality of participation and access to knowledge and information. 2. **Key sources of information:** key informants and meeting minutes. 3. **How:** interviews and review of any documents. 4. **Comments:** relates to community dynamism and power relations.

Were there particular groups who obviously did NOT attend either formal or informal meetings during: planning and design, implementation and post completion; if so, who were they?	1. **Why:** identify disadvantaged groups. 2. **Key sources of information:** key informants. 3. **How:** interviews. 4. **Comments:** disadvantaged groups may be denied access to the procurement process. This indicator will help in identifying such groups.
Rank score the level of participation during: planning and design, implementation and post completion by: • **Male** • **Female** • **Other groups (e.g.)** **[Score 20 maximum and 10 minimum].**	1. **Why:** quality assessments of the community participation in the meetings. 2. **Key sources of information:** key informants. 3. **How:** interviews. 4. **Comments:** this provides an indication of who participates in meetings.
Rank score the atmosphere of the meetings during: planning and design, implementation and post completion [20 is the most comfortable and 10 the most uncomfortable].	1. **Why:** quality assessment of community participation in the meetings. 2. **Key sources of information:** key informants and minutes of meetings. 3. **How:** interviews and review of any documents. 4. **Comments:** this provides an indication of how comfortable the community members were in the meetings.

...continued

Indicator	Description
Rough percentage of the time taken by the community discussing issues in meeting during: planning and design, implementation and post completion related to: • information/knowledge sharing; • negotiation on contracts; • disputes; • others.	1. **Why:** quality assessment of community meetings; what do they discuss, who discusses and how. 2. **Key sources of information:** key informants and minutes of meetings. 3. **How:** interviews and review of any documents. 4. **Comments:** this relates to wider aspects of social impacts.
Number of meetings with the disadvantaged groups during: planning and design, implementation and post completion. The groups should be identified.	1. **Why:** access of disadvantaged groups. 2. **Key sources of information:** key informants and project files. 3. **How:** interviews and review of the documents. 4. **Comments:** this identifies any special care taken to take into account the requirements of disadvantaged groups.
Time taken for any relevant approval from donors, if applicable during: planning and design, implementation and post completion.	1. **Why:** this relates to the efficiency of donors in the procurement process. 2. **Key sources of information:** project files.

	3. **How:** determine the dates when the project sent documents for approval and when they were returned from the donor's offices. Determine the difference between the dates. 4. **Comments:** in many cases the delivery time of infrastructure is affected by delays by the donors.
Time elapsed from first community meeting to the approval of works for implementation. Who were involved in the approval cycle?	1. **Why:** this indicates the delivery time as perceived by the community. 2. **Key sources of information:** key informants and project files. 3. **How:** interviews and review of the documents. 4. **Comments:** community or users are not interested in who is delaying the delivery of services in the supply chain. For them it is either on time or not. Their expectation clock starts when an agreement is reached with the community about the delivery of infrastructure. Consumer satisfaction is essential in delivery of urban services. One element for such satisfaction is a short delivery time along with excellent quality.
Incidences of community expressing interest in playing an active role in the community partnered procurement during: planning and design, implementation and post completion.	1. **Why:** community initiatives. 2. **Key sources of information:** key informants. 3. **How:** interviews. 4. **Comments:** indicates the motivation of the community to participate.

...continued

Indicator	Description
Number of works vetted by the community. Who were involved in those meetings during: planning and design, implementation and post completion(men, women, other groupings).	1. **Why:** community participation in reviewing the works and services. 2. **Key sources of information:** project files and key informants. 3. **How:** interviews and review of the documents. 4. **Comments:** power relations, related to the role of the community in approval of works and services.
Number of organizations or departments or agencies involved.	1. **Why:** complexity of organizational design. 2. **Key sources of information:** project files and key informants. 3. **How:** review of the documents and interviews. 4. **Comments:** co-ordination may be a desired element in a development project but may be hard to achieve.
Number of incidences of Monitoring meetings with the community. Who were involved in those meetings during: planning and design, implementation and post completion?	1. **Why:** community participation in monitoring. 2. **Key sources of information:** project files and key informants. 3. **How:** review of the documents and interviews. 4. **Comments:** if the community is taken as a partner their perceptions are the critical element. This relates to power relations.

Number of incidences of Evaluation meetings with the community. Who were involved in those meetings?	1. **Why:** community participation in evaluation. 2. **Key sources of information:** project files and key informants. 3. **How:** review of the documents and interviews. 4. **Comments:** if the community is taken as a partner their perceptions are the critical element. This relates to power relations.
Rank score the potential for community organization around some other issue as a result of the community partnered procurement [20 is maximum and 10 is minimum potential].	1. **Why:** indirect impact of procurement on capacity building. 2. **Key sources of information:** project information and key informants. 3. **How:** review of the documents and interviews. 4. **Comments:** community organization which resulted as a consequence of procurement can be used for other development related activities.
Rank score the attitude of officials to co-operate at a working level with other sections, departments or organizations [20 is maximum co-operation and 10 is minimum].	1. **Why:** indirect impact of procurement on changes in attitudes of officials. 2. **Key sources of information:** key informants and project personnel. 3. **How:** interviews. 4. **Comments:** working in community partnered procurement engenders positive attitudinal changes towards co-operation with other sections such as community development and health.
Rank score the attitude of officials to co-operate/partner with community [20 is maximum partnering relation and 10 is minimum].	1. **Why:** indirect impact of procurement on changes in attitudes of officials. 2. **Key sources of information:** key informants and project officials. 3. **How:** interviews. 4. **Comments:** working in community partnered procurement engenders positive attitudes towards community.

Part-C. Socio-economic issues (enterprise development, poverty alleviation and empowerment)

Table 3.6. Socio-economic indicators

Indicator	Description
Number of community labour days (unskilled). • **Male** • **Female**	1. **Why:** indirect financial benefit to community. 2. **Key sources of information:** project files and key informants. 3. **How:** review of the documents and interviews. 4. **Comments:** circulation of money in the local economy.
Number of community labour days (skilled). • **Male** • **Female**	1. **Why:** indirect financial benefit to community. 2. **Key sources of information:** project files and key informants. 3. **How:** review of the documents and interviews. 4. **Comments:** circulation of money in the local economy.
Were the same people involved or the people changed on different occasions (for both skilled and unskilled workers)?	1. **Why:** access of the community to work. 2. **Key sources of information:** project files and key informants. 3. **How:** interviews and review of the documents. 4. **Comments:** to identify any monopoly which also relates to power relationships.

Number of days training provided in skills development related to procurement of infrastructure. • Formal • Informal	1. **Why:** quantifying the training provided and mechanisms for training. 2. **Key sources of information:** project files. 3. **How:** review of the documents. 4. **Comments:** an indirect benefit of infrastructure provision may be community development through procurement.
How many women were trained?	1. **Why:** identification and quantification of skills development for women. 2. **Key sources of information:** key informants and project files. 3. **How:** interviews and review of the documents. 4. **Comments:** access of women to work and skills development.
Who provided the training?	1. **Why:** power relations and mechanisms of training provision. 2. **Key sources of information:** key informants and project files. 3. **How:** interviews and review of the documents. 4. **Comments:** this relates to human resources development.
Who received the training?	1. **Why:** to monitor transparency in provision of training. 2. **Key sources of information:** key informants and project files. 3. **How:** interviews and review of the documents. 4. **Comments:** identification of any disadvantaged groups such as women.

...continued

Indicator	Description
Nature of training, for example 'on the job' or classroom.	1. **Why:** to monitor the nature of frequently provided training. 2. **Key sources of information:** key informants and project files. 3. **How:** interviews and review of the documents. 4. **Comments:** in many cases 'on the job' training is frequently provided but not recognized. Identifying such training may lead to further improvements.
Has training led to any formally recognized qualification?	1. **Why:** linkage with formal systems. 2. **Key sources of information:** Education department documents and key informants. 3. **How:** interviews and review of the documents. 4. **Comments:** some professional development training provided may be linked with the formal systems. In many cases the informal system is catering for the real requirement of the micro-contractors.
Was training perceived to be useful by the trainee?	1. **Why:** perception of trainee, attitude related. 2. **Key sources of information:** key informants. 3. **How:** interviews. 4. **Comments:** this relates to the perceived usefulness of the training by the trainee.

Any incidence of training by the trained?	1. **Why:** relates to aspects of human resources development. 2. **Key sources of information:** project files and key informants. 3. **How:** interviews and review of the documents. 4. **Comments:** important secondary impact widening the overall benefits.
Incidences of those acquired skills being used.	1. **Why:** relates to aspects of human resources development. 2. **Key sources of information:** project files and key informants. 3. **How:** interviews and review of the documents. 4. **Comments:** community organizations are learning organizations. This indicator tries to capture some evidence of this.
Number of incidences of existing or new enterprises developed due to infrastructure provision or related activities. Examples could be emergence of commercial contractors, emergence of suppliers, canteen shops etc.	1. **Why:** identification and exploration of indirect impacts of urban infrastructure procurement. 2. **Key sources of information:** key informants, project files. 3. **How:** interviews and review of the documents. 4. **Comments:** community partnered procurement processes support and encourage enterprise development. Circulation of money in local economy.

...continued

Indicator	Description
What are the economic impacts of the infrastructure provision through community partnered procurement. Examples could be increase in the sales of the hardware shop, increase in the sales of the local material supplier.	1. **Why:** identification and exploration of indirect impacts of urban infrastructure procurement. 2. **Key sources of information:** key informants and survey. 3. **How:** interviews. 4. **Comments:** infrastructure provision generates or encourages activities that will have a positive impact on the economy of the community. Circulation of money in local economy.
How people were involved at what wage rates as compared to the market rates and for how long.	1. **Why:** monitor any exploitation of community. 2. **Key sources of information:** survey, national wage rate and project files. 3. **How:** review of documents and interviews. 4. **Comments:** community partnered procurement is not about getting cheap labour or providing inferior quality work. The community should be remunerated as per the value of their contribution.
Any impact on the employment of women?	1. **Why:** monitoring the access of women to opportunities. 2. **Key sources of information:** project files and key informants. 3. **How:** review of the documents and interviews. 4. **Comments:** This may also bring in cultural values related to working women in some countries.

Any impact on the ability to earn from home or community based activities ?	1. **Why:** indirect economic impact. 2. **Key sources of information:** key informants. 3. **How:** interviews. 4. **Comments:** infrastructure provision improves the ability to earn more in terms of time saving and improved services like access.
Any incidences of increase in property values or rents?	1. **Why:** monitor and evaluate direct and indirect impacts of urban infrastructure provision. 2. **Key sources of information:** surveys and key informants. 3. **How:** interviews. 4. **Comments:** relates to the indirect financial benefits to the poor of owning assets and an indication of better quality of life in the area.
Incidences in improvement of social relations due to the process or the product of the infrastructure procurement.	1. **Why:** monitor and evaluate direct and indirect impacts of urban infrastructure provision. 2. **Key sources of information:** key informants. 3. **How:** interviews. 4. **Comments:** this relates to the impact on social relations within and with other communities.

...continued

Indicator	Description
Incidences of saving of time due to infrastructure provision.	1. **Why:** monitor and evaluate direct and indirect impacts of urban infrastructure provision. 2. **Key sources of information:** key informants. 3. **How:** interviews. 4. **Comments:** this relates to financial, economic and social dimensions of impacts. Quantification of the benefits may be undertaken later on.
Incidences of empowerment, ability to choose, access to the officials , access to decision making process.	1. **Why:** power sharing with community. 2. **Key sources of information:** key informants and contract procedures. 3. **How:** interviews and review of the documents. 4. **Comments:** this relates to the linkage between different roles and responsibilities and power relations.

Further information about the use of performance indicators

Comparing public and non-public sector works

Where the procurement process involves the public sector, the steps are well defined and documented. For example, it is relatively straight forward to calculate how long, on average, the system is taking to issue a works order after tender invitation by obtaining the relevant dates from the contract files. In comparison to the well defined public sector procurement process, the process in other than the public sector is hard to trace. The problems are greater in informal processes. Interestingly, the terms used may be different, or in some cases the steps involved may not be named, however there is a parallel sequence of events to those in the public sector. The guiding principle here is not to be fixated on terms but to look for the sequences and the milestones. Note that indicators such as the number of community labour days generated by micro-contracts are also useful in non-community partnered works.

Further analysis

Once general problems have been identified, the indicators can be used to explore the problems in more detail. For example, if the time taken from approval to the contract stage (TL6) indicates that this process is taking longer than anticipated, carry out further analysis using additional indicators to determine the amount of time taken at each stage of the pre-contract process (TL1, TL11 and TL16 for example). This may show that delays are occurring primarily during the tender approval process, which in turn could be due to deficiencies in performance of the official responsible.

Handling information

Prepare a simple worksheet for collection of data. The use of a spreadsheet is desirable, though not essential, to speed up the data management and analysis. We have used SPSS(Statistical Package for Social Sciences) and found it extremely valuable for data analysis.

Management information systems (MIS) of appropriate size can be a very useful tool, however, they can soon become unwieldy if too much information is collected; this in turn may result in late reports to the decision makers. The size of the MIS should be such that the users can easily access it and select the information required. Data related to 100 contracts can easily be handled at a Junior Engineer or equivalent level. Another option is to have a simple summary of indicators, updated regularly, and filed with each contract.

Looking for further details

The indicators for cost growth (R1) and time growth (R2) deal with the variations in the cost and time compared to the initial contract values. Some users have suggested that the causes of such growth should also be explored. However, it is essential to identify the key problem areas before causes and solutions are investigated.

There is no end to the degree to which the indicators can be developed, however there are costs and benefits associated with performance monitoring. There are clear implications for resources, time and money, the more detailed the information generated. Another important issue is the magnitude and management of this information. Too much data does not help managerial decision making. In the context of urban development the minimum information necessary to make appropriate decisions should be generated due to already scarce resources. In summary, there is a deliberate attempt to keep the information generation to a minimum level and leave the users with a tested methodology which may be developed further if required.

At present the indicators related to community involvement in O&M only identify whether there is any such community role; these may be further developed to indicate more detailed factors such as the amount of time contributed by the community.

Indicators dealing with the participation of women and disadvantaged groups reveal that in many cases, including community partnered micro-contracts, there was no specific action taken to ensure such participation. This is an important finding and suggests that there is a potential to further desegregate the indicators on gender basis.

It was found important to differentiate between the formal and informal meetings and training. In some cases users had difficulty in obtaining information related to informal training days. In these cases masons and community organizers have proved to be a valuable source of information.

Looking for trends

In the analysis of the indicators it is useful to see a trend in the performance of the micro-contracts. This can be achieved by using data related to many contracts over a period of time. Analysis of this nature is essential to develop benchmarks or yard sticks against which future performance can be evaluated.

Inter-linking indicators

Some of the Part B indicators identify the number of meetings with the community. The information portrayed by such indicators should be considered in conjunction with a number of qualitative indictors. One can have 20 community meetings but that does not necessarily mean that those meetings were useful for the community. The atmosphere, participation and impacts should also be examined.

Indicators in parts B and C managed to identify and assign some quantitative and qualitative values to a number of issues related to social and economic impacts, however some issues are inherently difficult to quantify by a single indicator. For example, it was reported that property values in some cases increased by between 6 and 20% as a result of infrastructure provision. Such information is relatively straight forward but to capture the full impact on empowerment, indicators relating to community organization, community initiatives, and community self-confidence, need to be investigated.

Section 4
Supporting evidence

Analysis of Group A Indicators

In order to test the proposed indicators, data was collected from urban local authorities, special projects and NGOs. A brief summary of the organizations and the contexts from which the data was collected is provided in Table 4.1.

The average cost and duration of the micro-contracts for non-community and community partnered contracts are shown in Tables 4.2 and 4.3 respectively. The contracts considered covered a relatively broad spectrum with average values ranging from only $152 to over $142, 000, and durations of between 8 and 244 calendar days. The contracts were related to a variety of works encompassing water and sanitation, access/roads, drainage, small buildings, and recreational infrastructure.

Data analysis: time and cost

A selection of core indicators from Part A have been investigated in greater depth. The mean values of these indicators are presented in Tables 4.4 and 4.5 for non-community and community contracts respectively. Only a small portion of the data collected during this study is presented here, however all of the data is available from the author if required.

Key to performance indicators selected for further analysis

Performance Indicator	Description
R1	Cost growth = Final contract cost/Initial contract cost
R2	Time growth = Final contract duration/Initial contract duration
R3	Lead time = Time required to commence works/contract duration
R4	Technical sanction cost/Engineer's detailed estimate
R5	Engineer's detailed estimate/Initial contract cost
R6	Engineer's detailed estimate/Final contract cost
TL1	Time taken from approval to Tender invitation
TL6	Time taken from approval to the start of the contract
TL9	Time taken to commence O&M after completion of the contract
TL13	Time taken from Tender invitation to the start of the contract

Table 4.1. Number of contracts used for development and testing of the indicators			
Organizational context	*Country*	*No. of non-community contracts*	*No. of community contracts*
Poverty related projects (Project Management unit and city level Authority) **(SIP)**	India	39	11
Colombo Municipal Corporation (Drainage and project division) (City Authority) **(CMC)**	Sri Lanka	85	
National Housing and Development Authority (National level Authority) **(NHDA)**	Sri Lanka		59
Clean Settlement project unit **(CSPU)**	Sri Lanka		11
Faisalabad Development Authority/Water and Sanitation Agency (City Authority and project Management unit) **(FDA)**	Pakistan	98	102
Karachi Municipal Corporation and Karachi Development Authority (City Authority) **(KMC/KDA)**	Pakistan	130	56
Sindh Katchi Abadi Authority (Provincial Authority) **(SKAA)**	Pakistan	53	28
Orangi Pilot Project (NGO) **(OPP)**	Pakistan		71
Anjuman-e Samaji-Behbood (CBO) **(ASB)**	Pakistan		56
Total		405	394

Table 4.2. Average cost and duraction of the non-community micro-contracts

Organizational context	Mean contract cost in local currency	Equivalent UK pounds	Equivalent US dollars	Mean contract duration. Calendar days
Poverty related projects (Project Management unit and city level Authority) **(SIP)**	530,358	7,577	12,122	156
Colombo Municipal Corporation (Drainage division) (City Authority) **(CMC)**	14,714	128	205	8
Colombo Municipal Corporation (Project division) (City Authority) **(CMC)**	553,796	4,816	7,705	76
National Housing and Development Authority (National level Authority) **(NHDA)**	10,254,182	89,167	142,667	229
Faisalabad Development Authority/Water and Sanitation Agency (City Authority and project Management unit) **(FDA)**	95,034	1,188	1,901	25
Karachi Municipal Corporation and Karachi Development Authority (City Authority) **(KMC/KDA)**	846,522	10,582	16,930	49
Sindh Katchi Abadi Authority (Provincial Authority) **(SKAA)**	404,724	4,761	2,976	93

Note: For monetary conversion factors see notes following Table 4.3.

Table 4.3. Average cost and duration of the community micro-contracts

Organizational context	Mean contract cost in local currency	Equivalent UK pounds	Equivalent US dollars	Mean contract duration. Calendar days
Poverty related projects (Project Management unit and city level Authority) **(SIP)**	52,520	750	1,200	53
National Housing and Development Authority (National level Authority) **(NHDA)**	383,420	3,334	5,335	76
Clean Settlement project unit **(CSPU)**	439,002	3,817	6,108	83
Faisalabad Development Authority/Water and Sanitation Agency (City Authority and project Management unit) **(FDA)**	35,780	447	716	46
Karachi Municipal Corporation and Karachi Development Authority (City Authority) **(KMC/ KDA)**	3,761,196	47,015	75,224	244
Sindh Katchi Abadi Authority (Provincial Authority) **(SKAA)**	313,406	3,918	6,268	74
Orangi Pilot Project (NGO) **(OPP)**	8,586	95	152	11
Anjuman-e Samaji-Behbood (CBO) **(ASB)**	9,394	117	188	7.95

Conversion rates:
1£ = 115 Sri Lankan rupees, = 70 Indian rupees, = 80 Pakistani rupees, = 1.6$

Table 4.4. Inter-group comparison average value for the indicators for non-community contracts

Items	SKAA	KMC/KDA	SIP	FDA	CMC
R1	1.07	1.00	1.04	0.97	1.00
R2	1.58	1.79	2.39	1.00	0.63
R3	0.54	1.24	1.80	3.85	20.26
R4	1.24		1.02	1.03	1.06
R5	0.78	0.97	1.07	1.01	1.04
R6	0.77	0.96	1.09	1.06	1.05
TL1	32	6.14	146	33	60
TL6	38	35	228	64	97
TL9		31	79	109	1
TL13	49	32	112	35	32

Analysis of the performance data obtained for the conventional contracts awarded by SKAA (Table 4.4) indicates that the final contract cost was, on average, 1.07 times the initial cost (equivalent to a cost growth of 7%). The average time growth indicator (R2) is 1.58 which can be interpreted as a 58% increase in the duration of the works compared to the initial contract duration. On average the organization was taking 38 days to issue the contract after the approval. It is useful to know the current performance of an organization in terms of cost and time of the contract. The organization can then set a target for improvements, and allocate resources accordingly. For example, if it is seen that the performance is poor in terms of time, efforts can be concentrated on reducing the time lags between the different stages. Any significant improvement in contract duration will result in improved provision of urban services.

By comparison, analysis of the performance data obtained for the community partnered contracts awarded by SKAA (Table 4.5) indicates that the final contract cost was, on average, only 0.67 times the initial cost (equivalent to a cost saving of 33% against the estimate). The costs have been

Items	SKAA	FDA	KMC/KDA	OPP	NHDA	SIP	CSPU	ASB
R1	0.67	0.97		1.08	1.15	0.92	0.86	1.12
R2	1.43	0.77		1.59	2.10	1.66	1.31	
R3	1.85	0.68			0.64	1.73	1.79	
R4					1.03	1.00	1.10	
R5	1.00	1.25	0.87	1.00	1.00	1.05	1.02	
R6	1.49	1.32		1.01	1.09	1.16	1.20	
TL1					40	28	75	
TL6	85	31			47	92	97	
TL9					25	17		
	16				57		115	

Table 4.5. Inter-group comparison average value for the indicators for

consistently over estimated; it is not clear why this should be so, however, it represents one area where improvements can be made. The average time growth indicator (R2) is 1.43 which can be interpreted as a 43% increase in the duration of the works compared to the initial contract duration. Time is again a problem area which can be targeted for improvements.

Similar analyses can be carried out for each organisation.

Data analysis: quality of work

Most importantly, there were no recorded instances of work being rejected on the grounds of poor quality. However, anecdotal evidence suggests that work done by micro-contractors is by no means free from faults; these either go undetected, unreported, or have no action taken about them; this latter point implies collusion between the supervising authority and the contractor. We have not been able to tackle this tricky issue in an objective way. Quality of work is the central issue for service users and one way forward is to try to ensure greater independence in monitoring. There are two useful ways forward.

- Involve the user groups more closely in the monitoring; this requires both basic training and agreement at the outset between all parties (client, contractor, engineer and users) as to the accepted quality of work. (See the section on Community Organizational Impacts in a case study on the wider impacts of infrastructure procurement on page 70).

- The user group engages its own independent engineer or technician to oversee and approve the work; this is currently happening as part of the moves towards decentralisation in Kerala, India. The State Government permits a user group to charge the cost of hiring an independent engineer to the project.

Analysis of Groups B and C indicators for wider impacts of infrastructure procurement

The indicators in Parts B and C deal with inter-organizational and socio-economic issues of community partnered contracts. The validity and reliability of the information generated by the use of these indicators will depend on the methodology and the research techniques adopted by the researcher. The responses made by community members and officials during the testing of the indicators have been analysed and the key points are summarised in Table 4.6.

Tables 4.7 and 4.8 present the information related to community labour days and the days of training provided as a result of the community contracts. A glossary of the statistical terms used is presented in Annex 1.

A case study on the wider impacts of infrastructure procurement

The indicators presented in Parts B and C can provide a valuable initial assessment regarding inter-organizational co-operation and partnership, and a number of socio-economic issues; however, it is important to remember that the data collected in this way reflects the views of the officials, NGOs, and other project operatives, and may not be the same as those of the end user. Depending on the outcome of this assessment, it may be desirable to investigate the views and perceptions of the community in more detail by means of a participatory impact assessment (PIA) at neighbourhood level. The following case study describes the outcome of such an assessment. Communities are not homogeneous and it is considered important to test the performance indicators in a way which captures the diversity of perceptions and opinions. The case study tests the relevance and workability of the performance indicators and methodology.

The initial checklist to provide a framework for discussions and interviews is shown in the box below.

Initial checklist for participatory impact assessment

- Identify the various roles played by different stakeholders (Promoter, Engineer and Contractor) at different stages in the project process (identification, formulation, planning and design, implementation and post-implementation).

- Disaggregate the community, being alert to the involvement of women at different stages of the process, and to the possible exclusion of groups such as poorer households, ethnic or religious minorities, tenants (as opposed to the property owners), and try to elicit whether all groups benefit from the output.

- What evidence is there of sustainability; for example, willingness of all parties to enter into these kinds of partnerships again, and on-going community organisation around other needs or issues?

- Is there evidence of information sharing and learning on all sides?

- Were there disputes and how were they resolved, by whom, and through what mechanisms?

- What was the process of approving and agreeing financing; if the community financed the works and was it affordable to all community members?

- Did enterprise development or opportunities for income earning result from the activities?

- Who actually did the work? Did the community hire contractors themselves, did they supervise them and access people for quality control? Did communities engage in labour themselves and if so, which members of the community? Did any of the community representatives or CBO members engage in works themselves and if so , what aspects of the works?

Focus group discussions were conducted in 20 localities in Faisalabad, Pakistan. They were organised with the help of community organisations and involved both community leaders and end users, with representation from both women and men. Discussions were conducted and recorded in the local language.

No attempt was made to rank different kinds of impact in order of importance for one or another particular group. However, the methodology would allow for this if it was deemed important, for example if there were contesting groups within a neighbourhood or if women and men in a particular community have starkly different priorities. What follows is a

Table 4.6. Summary of key points arising from the testing of the indicators

	CSPU	SIP	NHDA	OPP	PMU	SKAA
No disputes between the community and officials	✓					
No incidences of deviations reported	✓			✓		✓
No damages or penalties imposed	✓	✓		✓		✓
No specific meetings held with disadvantaged groups	✓		✓	✓	✓	✓
All works were reported to be vetted	✓		✓			
Incidences of enterprise development were observed	✓	✓	✓			
Different community people were involved	✓		✓			
Training was provided	✓	✓	✓	✓	Some	
- classroom	✓	✓	✓	✓		
- on-the-job	✓		✓	✓	Some	

Indicator	1	2	3	4	5
Training was used and found to be useful	✓		✓	✓	✓
The trained also trained others			✓	✓	✓
Payment was less than the market rates			in one case	in one case	✓ (Market rates used)
Employment for women improved			✓	✓	✓
Earning capacity for households improved			✓	✓	✓
Value of rent and land increased			✓	✓	✓
Improvements in social relations			✓	✓	✓
Saving in time			✓	✓	✓
Community felt empowered			✓	✓	✓
Work has not been taken over by any agencies	✓			✓	
O&M community responsibility	✓	✓			

Table 4.7. Community labour days per contract

Contexts	Maximum	Minimum	Range	Mean	Mode
SKAA Male unskilled	575	20	555	202	20
SKAA Male skilled	70	42	28	56	42
NHDA Male unskilled	40	15	25	26.11	30
NHDA Female unskilled	45	20	25	35.28	40
NHDA Male skilled	25	10	15	20.28	20
NHDA-Female skilled	50	20	30	29.17	30
SIP Male unskilled	500	115	385	299.75	115
SIP Female unskilled	300	85	215	165.75	85
SIP Male skilled	100	4	96	47.25	4
SIP Female skilled					
CSPU Male unskilled	50	10	40	24.55	20
CSPU Female unskilled	75	15	60	35.91	30
CSPU Male skilled	30	10	20	18.18	20
CSPU Female skilled	50	10	40	28.18	20

Labour days provide opportunities for income generation and provides an influx of money to the local economy. As an example, based on a typical situation reported:

- 300 unskilled labour days @ $2 per day = $600
- 40 skilled labour days @ $5 per day = $200
- materials purchased locally @ 40% of contract sum (say $5000) = $2000

This could result in an additional $2800 circulating within the local economy.

Contexts	Maximum	Minimum	Range	Mean	Mode
Table 4.8. Number of community training days and women trained per contract					
SIP Number of days training -Formal	2	0	2	0.25	0
SIP Number of days training -Informal	15	0	15	6	5
SIP Number of women trained	5	2	3	3.50	2
NHDA Number of days training -Formal	1	0	1	0.89	1
NHDA Number of days training -Informal	2	0	2	1	2
NHDA Number of women trained	80	0	80	42.17	30
CSPU Number of days training -Formal	3	1	2	1.73	2
CSPU Number of days training -Informal	8	1	7	3	1
CSPU Number of women trained	69	20	49	40.73	20

Training improves the capacity of the local community to manage their urban services. In many cases training also increased the number of opportunities for further employment and income generation. The increased organizational, managerial, financial, and technical capacities improve the chances of enterprise development at the local level. For example, some of the groups are now working as commercial contractors in areas outside their locality as well.

Note that it proved to be important to disaggregate 'formal' and 'informal' training, particularly in the community partnered works where significantly more of the training was carried out on an informal basis. A significant number of women benefited from the training in this way. This capacity remains within the community and has the potential to be channelled towards further development. In many cases, the community-created assets acted as social or financial "gearing" leading to further development works.

brief summary of the findings, pointing to the most frequently cited impacts and concerns around five key areas:

- Physical impacts
- Economic/financial impacts
- Social and cultural impacts
- Community organizational impacts
- Political impacts

A number of issues were identified within each main theme and are presented in Table 4.9. Whilst these issues are specific to the case study under consideration, they also provide a reasonable starting point for more general use. The completed transcripts are available from the authors if required.

Physical impacts
The perceived problems prior to the project were:

- muddy and often impassable roads; and
- dirty and stagnant water due to poor drainage.

The perceived impacts of the project are described below.

- Physical access to the neighbourhood had improved. Taxi and rickshaw drivers enter the area without fear of damage to their vehicles. This is particularly important to women and school-going children who, previously, were virtually housebound or risked getting filthy and wet if they left the area on foot during the rainy season.

- Improved sanitation and hygiene conditions were greatly appreciated. An important finding was that improved infrastructure outside improved not only the external environment but inside the home as well.

- Paving streets gave people greater pride in their neighbourhood and reduced the accumulation of dirt inside the house. This in turn has meant less housework for women and girls.

- Sewerage and stormwater drainage improved the stability and safety of buildings by preventing damage to the foundations of houses from overflows.

- The removal of garbage heaps had reduced mosquito breeding and therefore malaria. A reduction in other seasonal diseases was also noted, such as boils, coughs, scabies, rashes, diarrhoea, influenza and allergies, related to dust, dirty water and unhygienic conditions.

- The establishment of a grassed park in the centre of one neighbourhood was welcomed because of the better drainage it provided and the fact that it prevented people grazing buffalo there, which in turn led to improved sanitation.

- A key physical impact was that a clean environment led to a greater sense of pride in the neighbourhood and inside individual houses. A gender difference was discernible, with women emphasising their new found ability to keep their homes neat and clean and with men emphasising their greater preparedness to invest in their properties through maintenance, extensions and improvements.

Story Box

"When the street was katcha people were not properly caring for it, throwing their waste in the street .... The street was quite dirty but now everyone coming into the house does not carry mud with them so the houses are cleaner .... And now people are keeping their waste inside and almost 80 per cent have engaged the sweeper to collect their waste from their houses".

Source: Group discussion no 6.

Economic/financial impacts

The perceived problems prior to the project were:

- dirty environment evidencing deterioration and decay;
- people felt demoralised; and
- people aimed to move from the area as soon as they were financially able.

The perceived impacts of the project are described below.

- Infrastructure improvements have led to increased rentals and property values. There are fewer sales of housing and land as people no longer want to move out of the areas.

- Women were particularly pleased that they did not have to move, possibly because of the importance of neighbourhood networks to women who are more housebound and tied to the localities.

- Advantages for property owners often meant problems for tenants as rising rents now precluded poorer tenants from moving into these areas or remaining in them. Similarly, some small entrepreneurs had been forced to move out of the area due to higher rentals, although different trade was emerging, including more itinerant hawkers selling wares and services door-to-door due to better access. This was of particular value to women in a society where purdah or seclusion is strictly observed. However, the establishment of parks meant women could use outside space more easily and acceptably and this in turn had led to improved business for shopkeepers from whom they made purchases.

- People also found it difficult to assess whether wear and tear on their houses had reduced as they were strongly focused not on the acquisition of infrastructure but its maintenance, which of course has its cost in terms of time and resources. Women, however, were very clear that they had to spend less on washing and on cleaning their houses.

Story Box

"Before, almost every household was ready to sell their property and some other people at that time made investments and purchased property at a low price. But now no resident is ready to sell their property .... Now people even from the posh areas are ready to purchase plots, even at higher rates. The households who sold the plots before development are somehow feeling pushtawa (regret)".

Source: Group discussion no 14.

Social and cultural impacts

The perceived problems prior to the project were:

- people were habitually quarrelling with each other;
- people were facing serious problems due to the poor conditions; and
- people did not used to sit together.

The perceived impacts of the project are described below.

- The improvement in infrastructure has led to changing attitudes and social interaction for the better. Relationships have been strengthened as community members have sought to co-ordinate the development and maintenance of infrastructure in their areas.

- For all groups, the development of a park has helped break down social barriers, and provided increased leisure activities, particularly for women. Before, the nearest point for an outing was situated in the city centre about ten kilometres away. Now women enjoy that facility in front of their houses and meet with each other and discuss things together and this has brought a positive change in people. Children have a place to play and it was noted that young men no longer hang around street corners as they have somewhere to go.

- There was a great sense of pride that women from other areas came to walk in their park and social esteem was possible given that family ceremonies and celebrations could be held in the park and were not restricted to the close confines of individual homes.

- The self-help initiatives and involvement of communities in the planning and implementation of facilities has led to a great deal of pride and confidence, the development of a 'can do' attitude, and satisfaction with standards and levels of service. Significantly there was no comment from the women on these issues as due to socio-cultural norms they were largely excluded from these processes. Nevertheless, women appeared to be supportive, if passive, and were enthusiastic about the benefits provided by the facilities, particularly in relation to improved sanitation, living environments and neighbourhood level facilities.

Story Box

"Most of the time women were quarrelling with each other – there was a tension among the households. The main reason for that was the throwing of garbage and the disposal of wastewater outside. With all this improvement that have got relief …. People have started behaving in a friendly way towards each other …. Now people prefer to sit together for the solution of their issues.

This area used to be referred to as Azaab Colony (Hell Colony) but now people are calling it by its real name Shadab Colony (Refreshing Colony).

We used to feel inferior living in this area. Relatives and other family members used to curse us for living in this bad area …. Young boys felt ashamed to tell their friends their house addresses. Even rickshaw drivers sometimes refused to come to Shadab Colony or demanded more fare. Residents of other areas made jokes. Now the people of this area are proud to be residents to Shadab Colony".

Source: Group discussion no 1.

Table 4.9. Themes for wider impacts of urban infrastructure provision

IMPACTS

Physical impacts	Economic/financial impacts	Social and cultural impacts	Community organizations	Political impacts
1 Has the facility (urban infrastructure) improved access?	5 Has the facility resulted in increased rental value? Please give examples.	12 Has the facility resulted in positive changes in attitude of the people?	20 Has the facility facilitated the formation and capacity building of the CBO?	29 Has the project made people more aware politically?
2 Has the facility improved the sanitary conditions inside the house and outside the house?	6 Has the facility resulted in increased land and property value/s? Describe with percentage increase etc.	13 Has the facility provided more leisure opportunities?	21 Has the facility contributed and made community more empowered than before?	30 Has the project brought any change in local politician/s?
3 Has the facility contributed towards making the building/s structure more stable?	7 Has the facility resulted in more and frequent sale and purchase of properties? (Means people outside area are more interested to come to this area and local people are	14 Are people more satisfied after implementation of this facility?	22 Are the projects, implemented through the community, more sustainable?	31 Has the process for implementation of the project brought any shift in traditional leadership?
		15 Has facility contributed towards improved community	23 Has the project led to community groups carrying out additional work?	

4 Has the facility contributed towards making the houses improved inside and outside.

getting better value for their land/ properties.)

8 Has the facility provided new opportunities for business? Give details.

9 Has the facility provided more earning opportunities for outside hawkers?

10. Has the facility resulted in less expenditure on health treatment?

11. Has the facility resulted in less expenditure on wear and tear of services?

relationships and decrease in conflicts among community members?

16 Has the facility enhanced the self reliance of the people?

17 Has the facility improved the social status of the people?

18 Do people feel a sense of ownership for the facility?

19 Is the facility providing a chance for gender equality?

24 Are people more willing to pay, now, for the services to the line departments?

25 Are people more convinced about the participatory approach of the project?

26 Are people more willing to pay for projects on participatory basis?

27 Has the project provided an opportunity to the CBO/peoples to develop linkage with the line departments?

28 Are people, after implementing this project, taking local initiatives?

- Improved social status was recognised by everyone and this was directly linked in people's minds to area-based improvements.

Community organizational impacts

The perceived problems prior to the project were:

- people were initially reluctant to get involved because they lacked both confidence and trust; and
- women were neither welcome nor interested in getting involved due to cultural factors.

The perceived impacts of the project are described below.

- For the men, involvement in procurement provided a focus for community-based activities and interactions. Previously, people in the same neighbourhood were not known to each other and the focus provided them with an opportunity of getting together in common cause. This in turn built organizational capacity. This did not always take the form of a formal organizational structure even though people united in action. In other cases formal lane level organisation emerged and persisted through the implementation of works and for maintenance.

- Feelings of empowerment were expressed in relation to dealings with line departments in local government. Observing the results of successful and united action was the most powerful influencing factor.

- Women felt that they played an influencing role in relation to sensitising the men, particularly in relation to issues of sanitation. They also gained socially from increased interaction with other women and reduced isolation in the home.

- The relationship between community level involvement and sustainability was seen as important, particularly in relation to quality control. The fact that everyone was involved in monitoring quality at all stages meant that people contributed readily and were more willing to take care of the facilities once installed.

- A demonstration effect was evident in neighbouring colonies, where people were also putting pressure on contractors and government officials and the community was getting involved in supervision. Women from neighbouring colonies were walking in the new park and saying that they were going to put pressure on their menfolk to initiate something similar in their area.

- While people are more willing to pay for services they want and the quality of which they are sure about, there is still a reluctance to pay for services from line departments. Some people argue that as they have spent their own money in construction, the line department should not claim any further charges. Others are willing to pay for services provided the agency concerned provides better maintenance and satisfaction. For example, bills were not being paid in respect of one particular agency, which did not fulfil its side of the maintenance bargain, while bills to other agencies were being met. In this sense the community saw itself as empowered although it was acknowledged that there was considerable dependence on the activism and energy of the leadership.

- Although not altogether convinced by participatory approaches, there was enthusiasm for working together collectively. However, this did not stop people 'looking towards government for development'. Moreover, while people expressed willingness to pay for participatory projects, they acknowledged that it was sometimes difficult to collect dues. It appeared that people contributed most willingly to the capital costs of sanitation projects and the on-going costs of solid waste collection, through private payments to a sweeper.

Story Box

"In our society it is not possible for females to form an organization ... as far as males are concerned, the intervention certainly facilitated the process of forming a community-based organization. But women are not interested .... It is the job of their menfolk to deal with the situation.

With the laying of the first sewer line in one of the streets of the area, the people from other streets started work in their streets. Now about 80 per cent of the area is served by the sewerage facility .... The community has contributed 100 per cent of the amount for those lines".

Source: Group discussion no 5 and 6.

Political impacts

The perceived impacts of the project are described below.

- People were more politically aware and thought more carefully about how they cast their votes. One group of women said they used to follow their menfolk when casting votes but now listened to the recommendations of a social worker in the area. As a result they 'kicked out' an ineffective traditional leader and elected a new face. There was a sense conveyed more generally, that people in communities are more closely linked with local activists and have reduced their dependence on traditional community leaders who were perceived as commonly watching out for their own personal interests.

- Although there is a long tradition of trading votes for resources, people were now asking for 'firm commitments'. Their dependence on politicians as conduits to public officials had also been broken due to their liaising with line departments directly.

- Both at local and community level, a new breed of political activists have emerged who are organising activities around local issues. It is difficult to establish a causal link between this phenomenon and community involvement in infrastructure procurement. However, there may well be a synergistic relationship at work. Clearly people are willing to become active and involved around issues that will improve their environments and life chances. This in turn has led to enhanced political accountability and it is no wonder that local politicians are feeling threatened by community level initiatives. The challenge for development which is by no means politically neutral, is to find ways in which the benefits can be extended to the poor.

Story Box

Now we don't run after these politicians .... People are quite bold and can talk to leaders now ... they can convey their viewpoint to politicians. There is a change in the attitude of the politicians. They are not making commitments with the people as they know that the people will not spare him later on if those commitments are not fulfilled .... They are making statements very carefully .... In the recent local body elections there was a major change. The elected councillor is an ordinary man and he has defeated the traditional leadership. And the main reason for his defeat was his past performance. He used to get personal favours done and people who did not have the power to stop him had no platform .... People were just looking to these politicians to approach departments. We were believing too much in the leaders. The process of forming organizations helps ... it helps to break our fears. We are now approaching line departments directly and successfully and getting results.

Source: Group discussion no 12.

Annex 1
Glossary of statistical terms

Maximum   The greatest value

Minimum   The lowest value

Range   The difference between the greatest and the lowest value

Mean   The mean of the n numbers $x_1, x_2, ...x_n$ is $\bar{x}$ where

$$\bar{x} = \frac{x_1 + x_2 + ... + x_n}{n} = \frac{\Sigma x_i}{n} \quad for \ i=1,2,...,n$$

Mode   The value that occurs most often within a set of numbers

Reference:
Crawshaw J. and Chambers J. (1990) *A Concise Course in A-Level Statistics*, (2nd ed.)

Printed in the USA
CPSIA information can be obtained
at www.ICGtesting.com
JSHW012045140824
68134JS00034B/3265